W9-AVI-037

Independence Day

Molly Aloian

Crabtree Publishing Company

www.crabtreebooks.com

Crabtree Publishing Company

www.crabtreebooks.com

Author: Molly Aloian
Coordinating editor: Chester Fisher
Series and project editor: Penny Dowdy
Editor: Adrianna Morganelli
Proofreader: Crystal Sikkens
Editorial director: Kathy Middleton
Production coordinator: Katherine Berti
Prepress technician: Katherine Berti
Project manager: Kumar Kunal (Q2AMEDIA)
Art direction: Dibakar Acharjee (Q2AMEDIA)
Cover design: Tarang Saggar (Q2AMEDIA)
Design: Neha Kaul (Q2AMEDIA)
Photo research: Farheen Aadil (Q2AMEDIA)

Photographs:
Associated Press: p. 12, 13, 23
BigStockPhoto: joeygil: p. 10; Scott: p. 9; stevieg: p. 30
Canstockphoto: p. 19
Corbis: Bettmann: p. 7, 22; Burstein Collection: p. 8;
    Philip James Corwin: p. 24; Ariel Skelley: p. 18
Dreamstime: Achilles: p. 17; Chrisdodut: p. 11
Getty Images: Hisham Ibrahim: p. 21
Istockphoto: hartcreations: p. 4; Gilmanshin: p. 5;
    Njari: p. 26; Kate Philips: p. 15
Jupiterimages: Ariel Skelley: front cover; Comstock: p. 1
Photolibrary: Clineff Kindra: p. 14; David H Wells: p. 27
Reuters: Tami Chappell: p. 25; Yuri Gripa: p. 20
Shutterstock: BZ Photos: p. 28; Costin Cojocaru:
    p. 29; Scott Rothstein: p. 31; Taipan Kid: folio
U.S. Defence: p. 16
Wikimedia Commons: p. 6

Library and Archives Canada Cataloguing in Publication

Aloian, Molly
    Independence Day / Molly Aloian.

(Celebrations in my world)
Includes index.
ISBN 978-0-7787-4754-3 (bound).--ISBN 978-0-7787-4772-7 (pbk.)

    1. Fourth of July--Juvenile literature. 2. Fourth of July celebrations--
Juvenile literature. I. Title. II. Series: Celebrations in my world

E286.A46 2010   j394.2634   C2009-901924-8

Library of Congress Cataloging-in-Publication Data

Aloian, Molly.
    Independence Day / Molly Aloian.
        p. cm. -- (Celebrations in my world)
    Includes index.
    ISBN 978-0-7787-4772-7 (pbk. : alk. paper) -- ISBN 978-0-7787-4754-3
(reinforced library binding : alk. paper)
    1. Fourth of July--Juvenile literature. 2. Fourth of July celebrations--Juvenile
literature. I. Title. II. Series.

    E286.A114 2010
    394.2634--dc22
                                                    2009013084

Crabtree Publishing Company

www.crabtreebooks.com   1-800-387-7650

Published in Canada
Crabtree Publishing
616 Welland Ave.
St. Catharines, ON
L2M 5V6

Published in the United States
Crabtree Publishing
PMB16A
350 Fifth Ave., Suite 3308
New York, NY 10118

Published in the United Kingdom
Crabtree Publishing
White Cross Mills
High Town, Lancaster
LA1 4XS

Published in Australia
Crabtree Publishing
386 Mt. Alexander Rd.
Ascot Vale (Melbourne)
VIC 3032

Contents

What is Independence Day?

Independence Day is a holiday in the United States. It is a **federal** holiday. On Independence Day, people celebrate the anniversary of the day the United States claimed independence from Britain on July 4, 1776.

This girl celebrates Independence Day by flying her country's flag.

DID YOU KNOW?

People celebrate Independence Day on July 4 each year. The holiday is also known as the Fourth of July.

Fireworks thrill audiences on Independence Day.

On Independence Day, people celebrate the history of the United States. It is a day to feel **patriotic**, or proud of your country. People celebrate in many ways!

Ruled by Great Britain

Hudson Bay Company

Great Lakes

Province of Quebec

Maine (part of Massachusetts)

Claimed by New York and New Hampshire

New Hampshire

New York

Massachusetts

Rhode Island

Connecticut

Pennsylvania

New Jersey

Reserve

Delaware

Maryland

Virginia

North Carolina

North Atlantic Ocean

South Carolina

Georgia

East Florida

In the 1700s, Great Britain ruled the eastern part of the present-day United States. Back then, the United States was made up of 13 British **colonies**.

This map shows the 13 colonies.

DID YOU KNOW?

Native North American people have been living in the present-day United States for thousands of years.

The Revolutionary War lasted until 1782.

A colony is an area of land that is ruled by a faraway country. Britain ruled the 13 colonies. The people living in the colonies wanted independence from Great Britain. The Revolutionary War broke out in 1775 between the colonists and Great Britain. The two groups fought many battles. The colonists won after several years of war.

Declaration of Independence

Before the war ended, Thomas Jefferson wrote the Declaration of Independence. This document said that the 13 colonies no longer wanted to be part of Great Britain. They wanted to be their own country with independent states.

Thomas Jefferson wanted the colonies to rule themselves.

DID YOU KNOW?

Thomas Jefferson was the third president of the United States. He is known as one of the founding fathers of the United States.

People cheered and celebrated when the Declaration of Independence was read.

The colonies agreed to the Declaration of Independence on July 4, 1776. Each colony had representatives sign the document. Visit the U.S. archives at www.archives.gov to read some of the Declaration of Independence. Ask an adult to help you.

Early Celebrations

Boston, Massachusetts, held the first Independence Day celebration in 1783. This Independence Day celebration included military parades, the firing of cannons, and people reading the Declaration aloud.

Soldiers fired cannons on Independence Day to remind people of the war.

DID YOU KNOW?

In the late 1700s, several governors of states recommended celebrating the independence of the United States.

Philadelphia officials rang the Liberty Bell to call people to a reading of the Declaration of Independence.

Early celebrations in Philadelphia included special dinners, speeches, parades, and music. Sailors covered ships in red, white, and blue decorations. In Bristol, Rhode Island, soldiers fired 13 guns—one gun for each of the 13 colonies.

Making Speeches

Today, many people, including politicians, make speeches on Independence Day. They talk about the history of the United States. Politicians discuss how to make the country better. They often meet with people and answer questions.

President Barack Obama greets a supporter on Independence Day.

DID YOU KNOW?

Many Independence Day celebrations include a reading of the Declaration of Independence, just as it was read in 1776.

Senator Robert Byrd gives a speech on the Fourth of July.

Many of the speakers on Independence Day talk about **equality** and freedom. Speaking about these topics has been a **tradition** since the time of the **American Revolution**. People listen to the speeches and think about what is being said.

13

Decorations

This home shows off bunting and flags in honor of Independence Day.

Many people decorate their homes, schools, and offices to get ready for Independence Day. The decorations for this holiday are always red, white, and blue. Streamers, American flags, balloons, and **bunting** cover buildings and homes.

Some people dress up as colonists on Independence Day. Others dress up as soldiers who fought in the Revolutionary War. Dressing up helps remind people of those who fought for the country's freedom.

Uncle Sam's clothes are the same colors as the American flag.

DID YOU KNOW?

Uncle Sam represents the United States, wearing red, white, and blue clothes. Some people dress up as Uncle Sam on Independence Day.

15

The American Flag

Many people fly the American flag on Independence Day. It is a **symbol** of freedom and **liberty**.

A symbol is something that stands for something else. On Independence Day, some people wear T-shirts and hats displaying American flags.

People fold the American flag in a special way.

DID YOU KNOW?

According to the United States Flag Code, the American flag should never touch the ground.

Lights should shine on the American flag at night.

The government adopted the American flag on June 14, 1777. It had 13 horizontal stripes and 13 stars to represent the 13 colonies. Today, the flag has 50 stars to represent the 50 states. The American flag is sometimes called the Star-Spangled Banner.

Picnics

Many people have picnics and barbecues with family and friends to celebrate this holiday. Foods that are popular on Independence Day include hamburgers, hot dogs, potato salad, and corn on the cob. It is the perfect holiday for eating outside!

This family is enjoying a barbecue on Independence Day.

DID YOU KNOW?

Some people have picnics on a beach to celebrate Independence Day. Spending the day outside is a tradition.

Save your popsicle sticks and make an Independence Day craft.

The weather is usually hot on Independence Day. Eating red, white, and blue popsicles can help you stay cool on a warm Independence Day. Popular desserts also include apple and cherry pies.

19

Parades

Many cities have parades on Independence Day. There are many floats and bands in the parades. Adults and children march in the parades. Soldiers sometimes march as well.

Parade watchers see many flags in a Fourth of July parade.

DID YOU KNOW?

On July 4, 1976, people celebrated the 200th anniversary of the Declaration of Independence. New York City celebrated with a parade of tall ships.

20

Have fun by clapping to the music in a parade.

Washington, D.C. holds the National Independence Day Parade, one of the biggest and best parades in the United States. Hundreds of thousands of people watch the floats, marching bands, horses, giant balloons, and famous people go by.

Songs and Music

Some people celebrate Independence Day with music. Independence Day songs help people feel patriotic. A composer named John Philip Sousa wrote the music for "The Star-Spangled Banner," which is the national anthem of the United States. People sing the national anthem on Independence Day.

John Philip Sousa wrote so many marches, he earned the name "The March King."

DID YOU KNOW?

The lyrics to "The Star-Spangled Banner" came from a poem written in 1814.

People sing Independence
Day songs.

Music helps people remember the
importance of Independence Day. "God
Bless America," "America the Beautiful,"
and "The Stars and Stripes Forever"
are popular Independence Day songs.

Baseball

Some people spend Independence Day playing or watching baseball. Baseball is sometimes called America's national pastime. Major League Baseball schedules every team to play on July 4. The audience watches fireworks after the game.

Children enjoy playing baseball on Independence Day.

DID YOU KNOW?

Many baseball teams create special uniforms just for Independence Day. The uniforms are red, white, and blue no matter what the team colors are.

Fans enjoy a baseball game and patriotic music before the fireworks begin.

Baseball became popular after the **Civil War**. Today, it is one of the most widely played sports in the United States. Playing baseball has become an Independence Day tradition.

Fireworks

In the evening, many people watch colorful fireworks explode in the sky. The fireworks sometimes explode in time to music. The shows last for several minutes. Independence Day is a great day to show off dazzling fireworks displays.

Fireworks light up the night sky on Independence Day.

DID YOU KNOW?

In 2007, over three million people atten[d]
the Sunoco Welcome America celebrati[on]
in Philadelphia. During the week leadi[ng]
up to July 4, the city held many events
and many fireworks shows!

26

These children are watching fireworks on July 4.

New York, Chicago, San Diego, Boston, Washington, and St. Louis are cities that hold huge fireworks displays. One of the largest displays takes place over the Detroit River to celebrate Independence Day in the United States and Canada Day in Canada.

Take a Trip!

Taking a trip is another way to celebrate Independence Day. A popular place to visit is Mount Rushmore in South Dakota. It has the faces of four presidents carved into it.

Mount Rushmore shows presidents George Washington, Thomas Jefferson, Theodore Roosevelt, and Abraham Lincoln.

DID YOU KNOW?

In Boston, the week leading up to Independence Day is filled with concerts and historic activities.

It is free to tour the National Archives Building.

The National Archives Building in Washington, D.C., is another interesting place to visit on Independence Day. You can visit the Declaration of Independence in person! It is one of the National Archive's greatest treasures.

29

Learn More!

Learn more about the Declaration of Independence and the events that took place during its creation. Share the information with your family and friends and teach them why Independence Day is so important.

Have fun learning about Independence Day!

DID YOU KNOW?

In 1776, about 2.5 million people lived in the United States. Today, over 300 million people make the United States their home!

Make an Independence Day crossword puzzle or quiz to give to your family and friends. Make a red, white, and blue prize for the person who gets the most correct answers.

Visit www.nps.gov/pub_aff/inde/events.htm and look for Independence Day events near you.

Use some of the words in this book in your crossword puzzle.

31

Glossary

American Revolution
The war during which the 13 colonies won independence from Great Britain and became the United States

bunting Thin cloth used for making half-circle banners

Civil War (1861–1865) A war between the northern and southern states of America

colony An area of land ruled by a faraway country

equality Being the same in rank or quality

federal A form of government

liberty The state of being free or independent

patriotic Describing a feeling of pride in one's country

symbol Something that stands for something else

tradition A belief or custom that is passed on

Index

Printed in China—CT